D1416263

A Friend Is a Gift to Cherish

Bear Hugs

Art by
Gay Talbott Boassy

HARVEST HOUSE PUBLISHERS
EUGENE, OREGON

Bear Hugs

Text © 2002 by Harvest House Publishers
Eugene, Oregon 97402

ISBN 0-7369-0909-5

All works of art reproduced in this book are copyrighted by Gay Talbott Boassy and
may not be reproduced without the artist's permission. For more information regarding
art featured in this book, please contact:

>   Gay Talbott Boassy
>   474 Comanche Trail
>   Lawrenceville, GA 30044
>   (770) 979-8281

Designed by Koechel Peterson & Associates, Minneapolis, Minnesota

Harvest House Publishers has made every effort to trace the ownership of all poems and quotes.
In the event of a question arising from the use of a poem or quote, we regret any error made
and will be pleased to make the necessary correction in future editions of this book.

Unless indicated otherwise, Scripture quotations are taken from *The Living Bible*, Copyright ©
1971. Used by permission of Tyndale House Publishers, Inc., Wheaton, Illinois 60189. All
rights reserved. Verses marked NASB are taken from the New American Standard Bible ®, ©
1960, 1962, 1963, 1968, 1971, 1972, 1973, 1975, 1977, 1995 by the Lockman Foundation. Used
by permission. Verses marked NIV are taken from the Holy Bible; New International Version®,
NIV®. Copyright © 1973, 1978, 1984 by the International Bible Society. Used by permission of
Zondervan Publishing House.

Printed in China

03 04 05 06 07 08 09 10 11/ RP /10 9 8 7 6 5 4

Hugs to

With love

On

A Hug for You

HUGS…a cute, simple word that has the ability to soften the hardest of hearts and bring a smile to any face. All of us need them—none of us can do without them. They're comforting and thoughtful day-brighteners each of us loves to receive. Hugs warm the heart like the sweetness of a child's hand reaching for yours, like the thought behind a special delivery of a beautiful bouquet of flowers, or like the promise of an extra-big dollop of cream on your strawberries. No matter the form, hugs keep our hearts tender and reassure us that we are loved.

And who better to give a hug to than a precious and cherished friend? Let your heart be gladdened and take pleasure in these cozy hugs that have come your way!

For memory has painted
this perfect day
WITH COLORS THAT
NEVER FADE,
And we find at the end
of a perfect day
THE SOUL OF A FRIEND
WE'VE MADE.

CARRIE JACOBS BOND

You Cheer Like a Sunbeam.

Oh, the world is wide and the world is grand
And there's little or nothing new,
But its sweetest thing is the grip of the hand
Of the friend that's tried and true.

AUTHOR UNKNOWN

I awoke this morning with devout thanksgiving
for my friends, the old and the new.

RALPH WALDO EMERSON

We just shake hands at meeting
With many that come nigh;
We nod the head in greeting
To many that go by.
But welcome through the gateway
Our few old friends and true;
Then hearts leap up and straightway
There's open house for you,
Old friends,
There's open house for you!

GERALD MASSEY

8

Let me have a friend's part in the warmth
of your welcome of hand and of heart.

JOHN G. WHITTIER

There is no friend like the old friend

who has shared our morning days,

No greeting like his welcome,

no homage like his praise.

Fame is the scentless sunflower,

with gaudy crown of gold;

But friendship is the breathing rose,

with sweets in every fold.

OLIVER WENDELL HOLMES

Ah, how good it feels!
THE HAND OF AN OLD FRIEND.

HENRY WADSWORTH LONGFELLOW

Friendship is the flower of a moment
AND THE FRUIT OF TIME.

<small>AUTHOR UNKNOWN</small>

Friendship cheers like a sunbeam,
charms like a good story,
inspires like a brave leader,
binds like a golden chain,
guides like a heavenly vision.

<small>NEWELL DWIGHT HILLIS</small>

Friendship is a union of spirits,
a marriage of hearts,
and the bond thereof virtue.

<small>WILLIAM PENN</small>

A friend is dearer than the light of heaven;
for it would be better for us
that the sun were extinguished,
than that we should be without friends.

SAINT CHRYSOSTOM

When a man is gloomy, everything seems to go wrong;
when he is cheerful, everything seems right!

PROVERBS 15:15

It's great to say "Good Morning,"
It's fine to say "Hello,"
But better still to grasp the hand
Of a loyal friend you know.

EDWIN OSGOOD GROVER

Of our mixed life two quests are given control:

Food for the body, friendship for the soul.

ARTHUR UPSON

And though a coat may a button lack,
AND THOUGH A FACE BE SOOTY AND BLACK,
And though rough words in a speech may blend,
A HEART'S A HEART, AND A FRIEND'S A FRIEND.

WILL CARLETON

Two are better than one because they
have a good return for their labor.

ECCLESIASTES 4:9, NASB

More precious far than gold refined
Is friendship knit with heart and mind.
Gold may go its fickle way,
But friendship, tried, will ever stay.

AUTHOR UNKNOWN

15

The friendly raindrops lend their aid

To every blade of grass;

The flowers in all the fields are swayed

Where friendly breezes pass.

The brook that glides along the glade

Sings many a friendly air;

'Tis endless friendship that has made

The splendid world so fair.

SAMUEL ELLSWORTH KISER

Strike hands with me, the glasses brim,
THE SUN IS ON THE HEATHER,
And love is good and life is long
AND TWO ARE BEST TOGETHER.

EDWARD WRIGHTMAN

17

You Are a Silver Lining to

In friendship,

your heart is like a bell

struck every time

your friend is in trouble.

HENRY WARD BEECHER

Every Cloud...

God bless the heart of sunshine
That smiles the clouds away,
And sets a star of fresh-born hope
In someone's sky each day.
God bless all words of kindness
That lift the heart from gloom,
And in life's barren places
Plant flowers of love to bloom.

AUTHOR UNKNOWN

One never knows
How far a word of kindness goes;
One never sees
How far the smile of friendship flees.
Down through the years
The deed forgotten reappears.
One kindly word
The soul of many here has stirred.
Man goes his way
And tells with every passing day
Until life's end:
"Once unto me he played the friend."
We cannot say
What lips are praising us today.
We cannot tell
Whose prayers ask God to guard us well.
But kindness lives
Beyond the memory of him who gives.

EDGAR GUEST

Friendship adds a brighter radiance to prosperity
AND LIGHTENS THE BURDEN OF ADVERSITY
by dividing and sharing it.

CICERO

God is my helper.
He is a friend of mine!

PSALM 54:4

Kind words
are like honey—
enjoyable and
healthful.

PROVERBS 16:24

It is my joy in life to find

At every turning of the road,

The strong arms of a comrade kind

To help me onward with my load;

And since I have no gold to give,

And love alone must make amends,

My only prayer is, while I live—

God make me worthy of my friends.

FRANK DEMPSTER SHERMAN

The silver lining to each cloud;
A CHEERFUL FRIEND—GOD SEND TO ME
Such friend to find, such friend to be.

AUTHOR UNKNOWN

'Tis friends who make this desert world

To blossom as the rose;

Strew flowers o'er our rugged path,

Pour sunshine o'er our woes.

Let us learn to help each other,
Hoping unto the end;
Who sees in every man a brother,
Shall find in each a friend.

He who refreshes others will himself be refreshed.
PROVERBS 11:25, NIV

You Warm My Heart...

God put us all upon this earth
That we might serve His ends,
And then, to give the world some worth,
He made some of us friends.

AUTHOR UNKNOWN

Friendship is a word
the very sight of which
in print makes the heart warm.

AUGUSTINE BIRRELL

If instead of a gem, or even a flower,

we should cast the gift of rich thought

into the heart of a friend—that would

be giving as the angels give.

GEORGE MACDONALD

Friendship is the essence and the aroma of life,
distilled from human hearts that find in each other the
understanding of the other's needs.
It is this understanding that opens wide the doors
of friendship and lets the heart pass through.

EDWIN OSGOOD GROVER

A TRUE FRIEND

Commend to me that generous heart

Which, like the pine on high,

Uplifts the same unvarying brow

To every change of sky;

Whose friendship does not fade away

When wintry tempests blow,

But like the winter's icy crown,

Looks greener through the snow....

AUTHOR UNKNOWN

Friendship is a chain of gold

Shaped in God's all perfect mold,

Each link a smile, a laugh, a tear,

A grip of the hand, a word of cheer.

As steadfast as the ages roll

Binding closer soul to soul;

No matter how far, or heavy the load—

Sweet is the journey on friendship's road.

J.B. DOWNIE

Be completely humble and gentle;
BE PATIENT, BEARING WITH
one another in love.

EPHESIANS 4:2, NIV

Oh friends whose hearts still keep their prime,
Whose bright example warms and cheers,
You teach us how to smile at Time,
And set to music all his years.

JOHN GREENLEAF WHITTIER

FRIENDSHIP—OUR FRIENDSHIP—
is like the beautiful shadows of evening,
SPREADING AND GROWING TILL LIFE
and its light pass away.

MICHAEL VITKOVICS

You Accept Me for Who I Am

A friend should bear
his friend's infirmities.

SHAKESPEARE

If your friend has got a heart,
There is something fine in him;
Cast away his darker part,
Cling to what's divine in him.

AUTHOR UNKNOWN

Blessed are they who have

the gift of making friends,

for it is one of God's best gifts.

It involves many things,

but above all,

the power of going

out of one's self

and appreciating what is noble

and loving in another.

THOMAS HUGHES

Happiness comes to those who are fair to others and are always just and good. PSALM 106:3

BEAR HUGS

COZY EXPRESSIONS
OF AFFECTION

623

Bear Hugs

OPEN 10 to 6

Love knows no reserve.

It never grows weary.

It counts nothing a sacrifice.

Its highest joy is in self-surrender.

It gives gladly. It accepts reluctantly.

Better, it says, to wear out

in self-forgetting toil

than to live long

in complacent self-indulgence.

AUTHOR UNKNOWN

My friend is not perfect—
NO MORE AM I—
and so we suit each other admirably!

AUTHOR UNKNOWN

I must feel pride in my friend's accomplishments

as if they were mine, and a property in his virtues.

I feel as warmly when he is praised....

RALPH WALDO EMERSON

Continue to love each other
with true brotherly love.

HEBREWS 13:1

I don't meddle

with what my friends believe

or reject, any more

than I ask whether

they are rich or poor;

I love them.

JAMES RUSSELL LOWELL

If there has come to us the miracle of friendship;
if there is a soul to which our soul has been drawn,
it is surely worthwhile being loyal and true.

HUGH BLACK

What deed or merit has been mine

That God to me should send

Of all His gifts, the most divine,

My other soul—a friend?

AUTHOR UNKNOWN

Our chief want in life is somebody
WHO SHALL MAKE US DO WHAT WE CAN.
This is the service of a friend.

RALPH WALDO EMERSON

You Are a Gift I Will
Always Cherish...

Friend is a word of royal tone;

Friend is a poem all alone.

A PERSIAN POET

You are sweeter
than honey.

PLAUTUS

A FRIEND

A friend is a present you give yourself—
That's one of my old-time songs—
So I put *you* down with the best of them
For you're where the best belongs.
Among the gifts I have given to me
Most comforting tried and true,
The one that I oftenest think about
Is my gift to myself of You!

CARRIE JACOBS BOND

My old friend
Makes my hopes of clearer light,
And my faith of surer sight,
And my soul a purer white,
My old friend.

JAMES WHITCOMB RILEY

There is in friendship the golden thread
that ties the hearts of all the world.

JOHN EVELYN

The songbird seeks its nest,

The sun sinks in the west—

And kindly thoughts

are speeding out to you.

May joy with you abide,

May hope be ever your guide,

And love protect you,

all life's journey through.

BURNSIDE

For the sake of
MY BROTHERS AND MY FRIENDS,
I will now say,
"MAY PEACE BE WITHIN YOU."

PSALM 122:8, NASB

Piglet sidled up behind Pooh.
"Pooh," he whispered.
"Yes, Piglet?"
"Nothing," said Piglet, taking Pooh's paw.
I just wanted to be sure of you."

A. A. MILNE
Winne-the-Pooh